TASTE
THE
ROUGHNESS

Kelvin Caribbean Lunch Club talking memories

TASTE THE ROUGHNESS

Edited by Christine Gregory
Published by Kelvin Caribbean Luncheon Club Publishing Project
c/o Kelvin Detached Youth Work Base, 205 Kelvin Walk,
Kelvin Flats, Sheffield S6 3ET.

ISBN: 0 9518555 0 6

© *Kelvin Caribbean Luncheon Club Publishing Project 1991*

Cover photo: Naomi Ramsey
Photos by Christine Gregory
Design, typesetting and layout by Susan Backhouse
Cover design and printing by Sheffield Women's Printing Co-op (TU) Ltd.
(0742) 753180

*This book is dedicated
to our dear friend Naomi Ramsey,
who died in July 1991*

"Everybody had to taste the roughness. That's how you pass the test. If you didn't stick it, 'Ya don't want to work.' What they say, 'Ya don't want to work.'"

Irene Maddon

CONTENTS

Kelvin Caribbean Luncheon Club — 8
About This Book — 9
Who We Are — 11
Acknowledgements — 13

1. *It's Me Mother Country* Arriving in Britain — 15
Irene Maddon, Ken Baugh, Naomi Ramsey, Hortense Baugh, Rastan Reynolds

2. *Some Of Them Came To The West Indies To Tell You To Better Your Position* Working Life — 29
Ken Baugh, Naomi Ramsey, Jenny Henry, Clinton Maddon, Hortense Baugh, Rastan Reynolds, Ivy Hines, Irene Maddon, Oscar Noel Phillip

3. *We Get The Rubbish* Housing Conditions — 57
Deleta Perkins, Ivy Hines, Jenny Henry, Naomi Ramsey

4. *You Were The Stranger That Came* Racism — 67
Ivy Hines, Rose Cummings, Naomi Ramsey, Irene Maddon

5. *Pouring Oil On Troubled Water* Our Children And Our Children's Children — 79
Naomi Ramsey, Irene Maddon, Jenny Henry, Rose Cummings, Ivy Hines

6. *Nobody Comes And Even Knocks On The Door* Retirement — 87
Naomi Ramsey, Deleta Perkins, Ivy Hines, Hortense Richard, Ken Baugh

7. *Home Sweet Home* Going Back — 99
Ken Baugh, Naomi Ramsey, Irene Maddon, Rastan Reynolds, Oscar Noel Phillip

Kelvin Caribbean Luncheon Club

Within the context of our work with Black young people on the Kelvin Flats, we became increasingly aware of the wider needs of the Black community, especially the isolation of elderly Afro–Caribbeans.

After consultation with a group of elderly Black people we opened for a trial run in December 1986. Our base was two small rooms and a kitchen in the Detached Youth Work Office — a converted two bedroomed flat on the Kelvin Estate.

In 1989 we moved to the Kelvin Day Centre because this could accommodate larger numbers and also offered disabled access. Although we are now looking to further develop the club, our main objectives still stand, ie, to provide a caring service; to encourage mutual support; to provide educational opportunities; to ensure that members are responsible for all decision making and hold all offices.

During the course of our work, members have shared their lives with us and we feel that their struggles and triumphs need to be acknowledged and valued by *all*.

Val Haslam and Vernon Collymore
Detached Youth and Community Workers

About This Book

This book is a collection of spoken memories and ideas, together with portraits of members of the Kelvin Caribbean Luncheon Club.

A while ago, I met with club members to discuss compiling an oral history put together from tape recordings of conversations and interviews. Over many months the contributors to this book talked about their experiences of leaving 'home' in the West Indies, arriving in England and finding work in Sheffield. They talked about their living and working conditions and the racism they faced in all areas of life. We also had discussions about what is happening in Britain today and how young black people continue to face racism in the job market and victimisation by the police.

After transcribing and editing, the outcome of our taped conversations is this book. It is the intention of all of us that the strength and energy of the spoken word should come through. The contributions are often in dialect. At all times they are as close as possible to words originally spoken.

Perhaps the experiences contained in this book will echo those of others and help to give a voice to the many who have ***tasted the roughness*** of working and settling in Britain.

Christine Gregory
Adult Education Worker, Loxley College

Lunch Club trip to Blackpool, July 1989

Who We Are

Hortense Baugh was born in Portland, Jamaica. She came to England·in 1960, living first in Birmingham for two years before moving to Sheffield. She has three grown–up children and three grandchildren but now lives on her own.

Rose Cummings was born in Barrow–in–Furness. She came to Sheffield in 1956 and worked as a bus conductress. Rose met her husband, Vernal, who is from Jamaica, in 1957. They were married in 1962 and now have a son and grand-daughter.

Jenny Henry was born in Clarendon, Jamaica in 1932. She came to England in 1960. After two years working as a chambermaid in London, Jenny moved to Manchester where she worked for three years as a hospital domestic. When she came to Sheffield in 1965 she worked briefly in a cutlery firm before going on to hospital and domestic work. Jenny was disabled by a car accident in 1987 and could no longer work. Most of Jenny's family live in America including her son.

Ivy Hines was born in Montego Bay in 1921. She came straight to Sheffield from Jamaica in 1957. At first she worked at Bachelors Foods but went on to work as a nursing auxiliary. Ivy was injured while working at Firvale Hospital when she was forty eight years old. She has never worked again.

Irene Maddon was born in Port Antonio in Jamaica. She has been in England for thirty years.

Deleta Perkins came to England from Jamaica in the early sixties. She worked in various factories in Sheffield until she was made redundant in 1983. Most of Deleta's family are back home in Jamaica and she hopes to rejoin them before too long.

WHO WE ARE

Naomi Ramsey was born in Barbados and came to England when she was twenty two years old. She worked for twenty years in the health service as a nursing auxiliary until she had a stroke that was permanently disabling. Naomi died in July 1991. She had two daughters, a son and three grandchildren.

Hortense Richards was born in Westmoreland, Jamaica. She came to England by boat on 13th August 1956. She has spent the last thirty five years in Sheffield. Hortense worked as a conductress on Sheffield Transport tramcars. She has done various jobs since marrying and having her four children. Hortense is now retired.

Ken Baugh was born in Portland, Jamaica in 1922. He worked on the family farm before coming to England in 1961. He has worked in the steel industry, for the gas company and the Council.

Clinton Maddon was born near Kingston, Jamaica in 1932. He came to England in 1960 and worked in Sheffield's steel industry until he was made redundant in 1981. He has two sons, both born in England.

Oscar Noel Phillip was born in Barbados. He came to England in 1961. He did various jobs in Sheffield including eighteen years at the engineering firm, Roper and Wreaks. He was made redundant from there in 1981. Oscar is married with five grown-up children.

Rastan Reynolds was born in St Elizabeth, Jamaica, where his father was a wealthy farmer. He came straight to Sheffield from Jamaica in 1962 and got work in the building trade. Rastan spent the rest of his working life in building. He is now retired and lives alone.

Acknowledgements

We would like to thank the following for their help with this book

Susan Backhouse, Black Community Development Fund, Vernon Collymore, Carmen Franklin, Val Haslam, Loxley College, Vic Middleton, David Peace, Joe Richards, Alan Sargent, Self Help Fund, Andy Shallice, Sheffield Arts Department

1

It's Me Mother Country

Arriving In Britain

It's Me Mother Country

Irene Maddon

Irene Maddon

"I leave a land of paradise that is Jamaica"

I leave Jamaica on 29 June and arrive July 9 1961. When I came off the boat and look around, I take my suitcase and went straight on to Sheffield. When I came here and see the place, I thought here was a land of paradise but when I think and look to myself, I know that I leave a land of paradise behind me that is Jamaica. I cried for three months straight. If I could have found the money at the time I came, I would have turned straight back.

I had to send money home to my mum and dad. I were twenty two when I came, that was twenty seven years ago. I've still got the same suit I came in, the one I arrived in, cream serge, and Irish linen. I let them out and they fit me now. I came on my own. There were lots of single women and men rushing in.

There were the sayings — 'It's me mother country.' At school I heard about England so I thought more or less it was a beautiful place. I never thought it was like this.

I never know house different from factory, because both of them was all alike, you see. Smoke came from the chimney. Sometimes I ran to a building and thought it was a factory to go and look for work — it was a house. When I turned to the house where I were living in Sheldon Road and see smoke coming out of the chimney, I was asking in the house what smoking meant and they show me the fireplace you have to make up to keep the place warm and it's from there I get to understand and get to know the difference between houses and factories.

In Jamaica we don't have to buy sunshine, we don't have to buy heating to warm we body, we don't have to buy clothes like coats and heavy jumpers and warm things like blankets and bedding. We came here, we have to buy them, so we couldn't make it to go back. And by debating and debating and debating we held up here twenty seven and thirty years because time works and works and carries on.

Ken Baugh

"I came for five years..."

When I came here I'd got a house prepared for me so it was all right. I got a job straight away. Gradually I worked and I pick it up. I was a farmer in Jamaica and when I came here I was a labourer in a gas company. I ended up as an operator. It was a big change for me, but it was all right really. I was right pally with these people. I can't grumble at all. I get along well.

In the 1950s they had it very hard, I understand that. I came here in 1961 and my brother was already here. Straight away I get me a job, I got twelve pounds a week. Yes, the money was nice. At the time it was good.

The first time I see snow in this country, I run out in the backyard catching it. A few weeks after, we run from it.

I came for five years, but unfortunately I didn't make it back. I go home after nine years on holiday. I go home four times now to Jamaica, but I still have the intention to go back home because I had no intention of stopping here so long. There is no special reason but 'Home Sweet Home'. At the back of your mind you still think that you should be at home. No matter if you get a thousand pound a day here and you're getting no more than a farthing there, there's nowhere like home. We all feel the same, but we couldn't make it back. Big rent, hire purchase, you had to pay everything out so you were never able to save the money in time to go back home. That's what happened.

It's Me Mother Country

Naomi Ramsey

Naomi Ramsey

"... the pavements were paved with gold"

I was twenty two when I came and I think Barbados was lovely compared to here. As I remember it, you chat to everybody. We were country people. You feed yourself out of the ground. If you get up in the morning you feel you want some potatoes to cook, then right, you dig up some potatoes. You want yam, then you go and dig up your yam. You pick your fruit off the tree. We had paw paw, everything. It was lovely.

When I came, they said, in England the pavements is paved with gold and we said, 'Well, we're going to England,' because there wasn't no money at that time. You had sunshine, yes, but there was no money. So we came to England to get money. But when you came it wasn't paved with gold, you had to work, work, work for it. It was full go go. I tell you, I came to Sheffield and from April I was walking, looking for work, walking backward and forward.

You could find the money to come but couldn't find it to go back.

My brother–in–law was working at Bassetts, working nights and he leave work in the morning and come home and he says, 'Oh, they're taking on people today.'

Before he goes to bed he takes me along and when I get there I walk in. They're not taking on no more Jamaicans, they say, and I come home. I say to Joe, 'What they talking about, no more Jamaicans? What are these Jamaicans that they're not taking?'

I couldn't understand it. All I knew was I'm Barbadian and I couldn't get work. In the end I got a job as a nursing auxiliary at Nether Edge Hospital.

Hortense Baugh

"It was like walking into a new world"

*I*t was like walking into a new world. Especially looking at these houses and thinking, 'My God, do people really live in those places?' We thought they were factories, not accommodation, nothing pretty about most of them.

We had our family to meet us. They brought us to their place and then when we got inside it looked a bit different.

Lots of times we came trying to find a job and we used to walk up to houses to look for one. You had to get used to that kind of thing.

At home we had such freedom, freedom of speech, freedom of the places you live and everything else. And then when you came here you have so many different people to go to, to tell you what you can do, what you can't do, where to go for what and that sort of thing.

A lot of people have found it hard. Some don't speak very good English and don't understand. We found we had a lot of problems.

I am disappointed but then I suppose the destiny of your life is what you make it. But you've got to be lucky as well as try hard and work hard. If you haven't got a decent job it's very hard. I've had petty jobs that just pay a little bit of money for bits and pieces and just ordinary living.

You were looking forward to something that would give you a decent life. You'd be able to save some money or even go back home. It's a lot of people's ambition but you get trapped in poverty. Poverty, it's nothing more than that, you can't do anything about it.

I think it was a big uprooting of yourself and your family to have moved away from home. The unwelcoming bit about it was the main hardship for some people. Where we came from everybody cared about one another. If you have any problems there's always sister and mother and aunties. But there was no one to turn to here, in England. It was not like it is nowadays when you have a lot of community work and social work that shows itself to you. You can't really blame the system now if you don't try but then there was nowhere to go. You had to try and sort it out for yourself and it was really hard.

It's Me Mother Country

Hortense Baugh

It's Me Mother Country

Rastan Reynolds

Rastan Reynolds

"I want to go back now and I can't go back"

I came in 1962 from St Elizabeth, Jamaica. It's a lovely place. I was up on a hill and I did see the sea four miles off. We have mango trees, a guinep tree and all kinds of different trees.

Me mum died when I was eight year old. Me dad died and leave two million pounds. He had acres of land. Me dad was quite a rich man! We had seven in the family. I work in Jamaica at all different kinds of jobs. We grew hemp to make rope. We plant banana, potato and all them things to make a living.

After the war, some of these people came to Jamaica and recruit we to England. They couldn't get nobody to work and came over here.

I were happy in Jamaica, more happy than what I been in England. I was twenty one, a young man. I hoped to come for work to get money. Money was over here, you see. And I come and work and get the money and buy a house, a decent house. I married in Jamaica and I sent for me wife. She a Jamaican white. I was living in a rent house till I buy my own house in Hillsborough. I buy the house. I fix it up nice and me wife leave me.

I don't feel glad I came here but I don't feel sorry. I want to go back now and I can't go back, I is sick, you see.

2

Some Of Them Came To The West Indies To Tell You To Better Your Position

Working Life

Better Your Position

Ken Baugh

Ken Baugh

"I was the one coloured man and they did give me a hard time"

I remember, I was working in the rolling mill at Hadfield's at Vulcan Road. It was all Rotherham men and I was the one coloured man and they do give me a hard time. They don't want no coloured man in that mill and they put me in it. Every ten minutes they stopped the mill. I could not do the job. I was just as good as them but they wanted to get rid of me.

I was a roller, back rolling. When they put me on that job first they were supposed to learn me. They wouldn't. At last I went to the foreman who said, 'Okay Ken, I'm going to learn you.'

I was using strength, so much strength on that job that you couldn't survive a week. So it's common sense you've got to use, and after that foreman teach me, it was easy. But they let me carry on doing it wrong fit to kill me.

It was a fourteen inch mill, rolling billets. The man in front gave me the steel awkward so that if I ever missed it, it was coming right on me so that I could have been burned up or something. He gave it to me awkward because he wanted me to get browned off so I'd leave the job. He did not want me on that job. He was just a labourer like myself on the mill.

If I dropped that steel and it cooled, it have to go back in the fire. I would get blamed for it and they'd say I was no good, 'He can't do the job.' But I never dropped one. At the end of the day I was trembling, I was that tired, worried, mentally disturbed. That's what they were doing it for. I don't feel good about those people.

One morning I came in for work right fresh and good, and we start to roll and then the manager, assistant manager and union man stand behind me. I don't know why. I found out the men in the mill had reported me to the office.

When we roll a hundred billet that we must, they take me in the office. They tell us how much time it took. The head roller had reported me for low production, and they prove it was a lie. But I survived! I survived until I leave it myself.

I was the one coloured man on the job and they did give me a hard time.

I take it hard but I'd got to continue because the money was lovely. I would never let them get topside of me. At that time there wasn't a lot of union around. I didn't complain to no one. I just stick it out and came out on top. It was a good paid job and they didn't want me to come there to earn what they earn, you see. It was just like jealousy, you see, but I understand. They was like that for a long time.

The management and union say we must get coloured in, and I was the first one. I did pay a high price for it. But I came out on top.

I stayed there for three years but production was going down and I pack it up.

It was a bit painful when you came. You didn't know no one, you didn't get any help and you have to find your way to work and back and it last a long time. It was a bit sad but you get over it. And then I started to enjoy it, I'd go out for a drink with my friends and then you feel on top of the world.

Naomi Ramsey

"Your qualifications are thrown out, you've got to start from fresh"

I used to do needlework at home. My mother sent me to a place where I learned to do dressmaking and on my passport is sewing. But when I came here sewing is different.

Back home I learned to cut without patterns and up till now I cannot cut with patterns. I can cut a dress. I can do anything without a pattern. I can cut it from my head. I can see a picture in a magazine and cut the dress.

You'd be qualified to do something at home all right. But when you come here it's no good. Your qualifications are thrown out. You've got to start from fresh, take what they give you.

We got no advice, no help, they don't want to know you. But then I went to Nether Edge Hospital. There was me and an English girl. The matron took her up to the office. When I went to see her she said, 'I'll take you on as a nursing auxiliary for three months for a trial.'

I used to go on seven to five at night for one day, the next day, ten till eight, and the next day, one till ten at night, and you go back the next day at seven. That was for four pounds something in the wage packet and when that three months was up she called us into the office.

She said to the two of us, 'If you want to do nursing you get less wages than what you do now and if you stop on as a nursing auxiliary you get that four pounds something.'

The English girl she said she'd do nursing so her pay was cut, she went down to three pound odd. I stop as a nursing auxiliary because I didn't want my pay cut. At the time I couldn't afford to cut my pay because my husband wasn't working. At the labour exchange they used to give him thirty shillings and from the time I get the job, they take it away completely and they says I'm working for enough to keep me and him. So that means I had to pay rent for the house, food and everything out of my wages. He didn't get nothing and I had to keep him. So I couldn't afford for my wages to be cut so that's why I stopped a nursing auxiliary till I leave.

That's why you stayed where you were. I regret that.

Better Your Position

Jenny Henry

Jenny Henry

"Oh Lord, Lord, I can't stick this job"

*W*ell, I came here in 1960. I leave Jamaica and land in England on seventh October. I came to London and lived there for two years. I get a job in January working as a chambermaid in a hotel in London.

Then I leave from London and I went to Manchester and stop there for about three years. I was working in Withington Hospital in Manchester as a cleaner and domestic. Then I leave Manchester and came to Sheffield. I'd got me family in Sheffield. I came over to live with my brother.

I got a job in a cutlery firm in Sheffield but I didn't like it. I never worked in a place like it before so I never liked it. It cut up your fingers. You had to rub the knives and things on a belt.

One day, the manager came and he says, 'I want you to do some buffing.'

I said, 'I don't know what buffing is.' So he put this big thing on, a big rolling thing with some cloth and I had to put the knife on and rub it.

When I do about a dozen somebody says to me, 'What's up with you. Why do you look like that?'

I said, 'What?'

She says, 'Go and look at yourself in the glass.'

When I go to look at myself, I was all over in muck and all sorts, and I couldn't tell meself different from the muck. I rush out and I start crying and say, 'Oh Lord, Lord, I can't stick this job, I can't stick it.'

I went straight home. I went straight home and I never go back, no never go back.

It's the first time I'd done that job and I says, 'Well, if a human being do that job and stay like that you wouldn't last too long.' It would go down your lungs and all over. They never offered me any kind of protection.

So I leave that job and I got another job in Lodge Moor Hospital doing domestic. After I leave from Lodge Moor I was working at Grosvenor House Hotel, and I work at Cavendish Hotel, then from there I work at Hallamshire Hospital, till I had my accident.

But that cutlery job, I can tell you it was murder. I never know somebody can work in something like that. I was mad because they didn't give it to nobody else, they says I must do it. The factory was full of workers and they put me on it. I don't know what they were playing at but, my God, it were shocking. It was disgusting.

Clinton Maddon

"Things just go right down the drain"

I come here in 1960. I come straight to Sheffield from Jamaica. I was a banana grower there. It was our own farm not far from Kingston.

I get a job here working at Brown Bayley steel works at Attercliffe. Is that place the World Student Games built on. That same firm I was working in, it finish. That why I leave there. The firm gone bust, made me redundant and everyone have to leave.

From that blessed moment, (1981), I don't work. Things is very difficult, was all right until then. Things just go right down the drain, everything flushed out.

Since the Conservative government is in power, is them smash everything up to pieces, burning out the steel firms, cutting everything, selling out the water, the electric, the gas. Everything they sell out. That's why we have it so rough now.

We is on the dump now, we is right on the dump. At my age I can't get a job at all. You go to a firm now, you tell them your age. They say, 'Sorry, I can't use you.'

You have to go back home. Even younger than my age have it difficult. The young ones, them feel it.

What we're getting from the DHSS is just hand to mouth

now. I have me mortgage. It very, very rough.

I never know that thing would catch me out at all. I lived down Attercliffe, that me first house. Not a beautiful house, but the Council step in and clear it. Give me a little bit of money, two thousand, one hundred pounds. I bought one up on Handsworth for thirteen thousand, five hundred pounds. The reason why I tackle that house, I were working at Brown Bayley's. I go to the Halifax Building Society and I get a tremendous borrow off them. Is that is cripple me till now. You pay, pay, pay for years. Life lick me so with money. I'm fifty eight now. I'm very sickly. I've got stroke. Me still getting treatment at Hallamshire Hospital.

Better Your Position

Clinton Maddon

Better Your Position

Hortense Baugh and her family

Hortense Baugh

"I'm still asking myself what I'm doing here"

When I left home, I was just from college finishing a commercial course and I had a job with a company. The starting money I got was fifteen pounds a week.

When I come to this country I took a job and I couldn't believe it. I took home four pounds from that job.

I'm still asking myself what I'm doing here. I'm not like everybody else. Most of my family are happy. My children might be happy but I'm not. I've never felt as though I want to be here.

Earlier years the chance was there to train but you know you can't just leave your family. I care very much about my family, they are my life. The first and foremost part of my life. It's hard to break away, it's just hard. I wasn't one who wanted to leave my child to go to work or go to college. I did try after that and got better jobs but it still hasn't been what I wanted. It still hasn't been good enough.

It's my fault really to be here and I'm not complaining about this country. It hasn't done anything to me, I've done it to myself.

Better Your Position

Rastan Reynolds

Rastan Reynolds

"Hang down your head and cry, Tom Dooley"

When I first arrived the place was a nice place. The country was nice. You see, I work on building. I come straight to Sheffield and I get a good job. I work for Gleeson. I work in Scotland and Wales and all over. I lay brick and do everything.

All my life I work on building. That me trade, you see, building and bricklaying. I'm a stone mason, I'm a finisher, I do everything on building. I pick up all that since I came here. I do building in Jamaica but we didn't do the kind of work we do here.

I enjoyed working in building. I was a tradesman. Not many black men work in the building trade.

I'm a friendly bloke. I get on with everyone. They call me Tom. They change me name. Me name Rastan, you know. Why them call me Tom? I was working on the building when I was singing this song,

> *'Hang down your head and cry, Tom Dooley.*
> *Poor boy, you're gonna die.'*

And I sing this song and they jump up and say, 'We're going to call you Tom.' And they call me Tom Dooley.

Better Your Position

Ivy Hines

Ivy Hines

"If you were dying you had to take Beechams"

I had been a nursing auxiliary at Nether Edge Hospital. I wanted to do midwifery but I didn't get through. I went to Firvale (it's now the Northern General) to work on the geriatric side. I generally worked on the female side but they transferred me to the male side.

It was a modernised block. At that time you had your own key and you lock yourself in and out. I was scared. We had to take these old men up the lift every night. I was scared because I thought, they're going to kill you one of these nights.

This night, second June 1969, I took them up to bed. One auxiliary was downstairs and there was only two of us on the ward. I was putting this man to bed and I could see him rolling his fist. I said, 'Come on, Clifford, be a good chap.'

After I said that I didn't know anything. I didn't know where I was. I heard as if somebody was saying a long way distant, 'Don't hurt her because she's only trying to do you good.'

I was knocked right out on the floor. I never recovered from the injuries to my spine. I never worked again from that night.

I had planned to go home to Jamaica for a holiday at the time. I was in the union and the union gentleman said, 'You can go.'

Well, when I came back I had what they called a delayed reaction. I felt very bad one night and the next morning I woke up and I were crippled from me head to me foot. They took me to hospital. I came out. They would not admit I had any after effects from the accident. I've been to tribunals but they'd never admit liability.

At forty eight years old I'd lost twelve years of me livelihood. I have suffered untold suffering, blackouts, everything. I've spent money on private medicine. I've been to Doncaster, London and then Birmingham. I wanted to get better to go back to work.

They said that there was nothing the matter with me, that it was all in my mind, until about 1973. I stood up and fell back and at last they said I have spinal spondilosis.

I've been through hell and back. I got no compensation.

When I was forty eight I was strong. I could swing you around. It's twenty two years now. There's not a part of me that's not altered. The social security did me in. When I went down to the medical board I thought they were going to finish me off. They said I was hysterical. All my body's been mashed up really.

But they always treated us bad when we were working. If you were dying you had to take *Beechams* and go to work in the morning. You could not be off poorly. If you were poorly at work you go to the duty room as if you're going to court. Just as if matron was a god. Regardless of how poorly you were you had to take *Beechams* and be out of that door six o'clock in the morning.

One or two became green frocks [1], but not many. We had family responsibilities when we came here. We couldn't train and lose money to get qualified.

Irene Maddon

"Everybody had to taste the roughness"

*I*t was eight pounds a week for men. For me three pounds seventy five. We work Monday to Friday from eight till five and Saturday till eleven thirty am. Three pounds seventy five for a week with all these hours each day. This was in Parkins, Scotland Street, in the cutlery trade. Chromium plating, cleaning tea pots and all those things.

There was all sorts of equipment and machines. Boilers one side, boiling all sorts of things, other side, machines. I'd never seen anything like that before and when I saw it was shocked. I'd seen the building outside but getting inside, it's a different thing.

In every factory there's a bad job. Every person they took on had to have a little taste of that bad job to see what type of person you are, if you would continue or not. Well some people stick it out until they took them off and give them a job. Everybody had to taste the roughness. That's how you pass the test. If ya didn't stick it, 'Ya don't want to work.' What they say, 'Ya don't want to work.'

You couldn't complain in front of the whites. We thought they'd tell the boss.

Some morning you get in, it were cold like ice. Especially when you go in a Monday morning.

As I came in the gaffer says, 'Irene go and clean those rods.'

I had to do it every morning because, I think, that I was the last person they took on at the factory so they get me to do it all the time.

When I'm cleaning it I feel really bitter. It go through me. It was like hot pepper or a dust, and that dust get in your lungs. I was sneezing all the time when I work on it. They took me off after a few days, then they put me on to working with this acid bath.

They tied up the tea pots by the handles and they dropped them into a big boiler with the acid in. And then you have to rub it. It's black and they bring it out and it's clean. You have to do it for hours. You do it till your shoulder hurts like fire and your fingers start to burn. You put on gloves and your gloves start to melt.

It was a dangerous place. I stopped there for three weeks. But before I leave the gaffer says to me one day, 'Irene, you're not doing enough work, you're not working fast enough.'

I says, 'Listen to me, love, in Jamaica we haven't got no factories. It since I came here I work in factories. So give me a chance that I can pick the job up. I can't just go down and shove myself in it. I'd kill myself.'

The man didn't like it when I tell him that, you see, and he points to the door and says, 'You can go.'

Better Your Position

Oscar Phillip

Oscar Noel Phillip

"Sometimes I do regret coming here"

I'm from Barbados. I come in December 1961. I didn't get no work, not before 1963.

I used to do a bit of work on polishing machines and washing machines, repairing them. After I was working at the railway on the Wicker. I didn't stop long at that job. I didn't get through the medical.

I had a job in an engineering firm, Roper and Wreaks. I work there eighteen years. I worked different machines, all sorts. Where I work I get on all right with them. I was the only black there at the time.

After, they get different managers. The last one there, he buggered the firm up and everything drop off. I got made redundant in April 1981.

I would say from the time *she* get in power everything went down. *She* got in power in 1979 and everything start to fall apart from there. It's the truth, anybody can tell you that, when *she* came, everything went to pot. It still not getting better, it getting worse.

I haven't worked since I got made redundant. I didn't get much money, they robbed me. After eighteen years I only get fifteen hundred quid. I was forty five and I got a family and all. No matter how hard I try I get nothing.

It been always bad for black people. Some of them come to the West Indies to tell you to better your position. But when you came here, you find something different. You can't get no work then because nobody don't want to know you. Now when you go for a job and say you're fifty, they tell you no.

My family, them all grown up now. There's five of them and none of them are working, I have two living at home.

Sometimes I do regret coming here.

Better Your Position

On the prom at Blackpool, July 1989

3

We Get The Rubbish

Housing Conditions

We Get The Rubbish

Deleta Perkins

Deleta Perkins

"This will kill me and I'm going back home"

Some people treated us well, some not. I think the housing conditions were very bad. It's hard to find somewhere to live. The white people that had houses, they wouldn't let it to the black people. Because they didn't think we was equal to them, we couldn't live in the same house with them.

It's always like that. The first black man that came to Sheffield, bought a house, then all the black people that come here get packed up in that house. One lot of people work all night and another lot in the days, and you share a bed. That was awful, really, because when you were home it was only family that slept together, not strangers and that was very hard to come to terms with. But when people start buying their own house, then they go from there and they could let to their family or someone they know until people start spreading all over the place.

But the housing conditions was the worst thing. I said to my husband when I first came, 'This will kill me and I'm going back home, I'm not staying here no longer. I'm going back home.'

We used to have our own house and go to our own beds and we don't like to be mixing up the way that we do. It was awful.

Even when you're cooking, you've got one burner to cook

rice, meat, vegetables, everything on one cooker. We used to have cooked breakfasts on Sunday morning, we had liver and we cook bananas and ackee and salt fish. We boiled banana and fried dumplings. A proper breakfast, that's what we had. And sometimes we had to buy bread and have sandwiches because we don't have a stove to make a cooked breakfast on. It was awful sharing.

Ivy Hines

"They threw stones all the time"

I was living in digs and I was really fed up with digs life and I had a friend who said, 'Hines, why don't you try and buy a house?'

So I found one. It were a beautiful house at Sun Street near Burngreave primary school. Very comfortable. Two big bedrooms upstairs, a little kitchen and front room. But my neighbours were rotten and they were stoning my house when we were sleeping.

I had to go to the hospital to do three shifts then, morning, nights and afternoon. They didn't like us. They threw stones all the time when I was sleeping. One man said 'black bambina'. That's what he called us when he were drunk, 'black bambina'.

So we really went through some rough days. Despite the neighbours I loved my house. But they started to knock down houses in Burngreave. I went to the Town Clerk. I says, 'How long will these houses be up?' He says, 'Ten years the minimum.'

I just finished paying me mortgage in May. In September I was out of it. I'd lost everything, really. All the money I'd earned in the hospital had paid me mortgage and finished it and after four years and six months I was turned out under compulsory purchase.[2] It was a very nice little place. They built flats there now.

Jenny Henry

"You don't know who's who"

I have been living at Roebuck Road. I've lived there twenty years now. It was all English neighbours and they were ever so good to me. They were all good, nice neighbours. All these neighbours moved out now, you don't know who's who.

Naomi Ramsey

"My home in Barbados was lovely"

*T*he houses were horrible, wet and damp and cold. In your bed you were shivering. You had to use three or four blankets. Sometimes you didn't have no more than one if you just came.

I lived in Brunswick Street, Broomhall. It was terrible. The digs they were shocking, indescribable. There was a kitchen and a bathroom and everybody just had to use them. In my room we had a little fireplace and we used to cook and everything inside the room. If you want a bath you'd bring the tin in front of the fire. It was the only way because everyone used the one bathroom. It was horrible. It didn't matter how big your family was, you had to live in one room.

The place I was living in was owned by an Indian man. He had two or three houses and in each one tenants had just one room. There were three or four of us in the same house. The house was a big house, there was one big kitchen and a bathroom outside. Everybody used to share them. It was horrible. It was cold and damp, it wasn't good. We had paraffin heaters in the room. They stink. We ended up in the worst housing.

Every time that you go to an English person's house who had a room, they turn you away from their house. They don't want you, so you go to a coloured person's house and you get it. But what the coloured people get at that time wasn't like the English people's house, they get the rubbish. It was a rough time in the sixties.

It's terrible, really, what we leave behind. My home in Barbados was lovely, a nice bungalow. You had your house and everything was there. Your water was there. There was no electricity, you didn't need it. You do as you feel like. You go where you feel like, you come back when you feel like. You do what you wants to do.

We Get The Rubbish

Playing dominoes at the lunch club

4

You Were The Stranger That Came

Racism

You Were The Stranger That Came

Ivy Hines and her friend Joyce Marsh

Ivy Hines

"Children of the Empire, listen to the call"

I think it's a different culture here. I think we've done everso well to cope, really.

It really surprised us to see the friction between the coloured and the white. We didn't know the name 'coloured'. We know we're Jamaicans. In England it's the first time we hear 'coloured'. We never had no hassle at all with the whites at home. And we have what we call the 'mulatto', the white man's children, they call them half caste here.

We had no hassle at all, that's the truth. They please themselves, we please ourself. That's what shocked me.

The main cause of the thing is education. We have been educated to believe that England is our mother country. We had history books about England. We all had to say, 'Children of the Empire, listen to the call.' We were England's children. England was our mother country and we know everything about it. Our mother country knew nothing about us! And that's what has caused the whole set up.

I blame the politicians because they made sure that we were taught in school about English people and the English people don't know anything about us. Just imagine that. If they were taught sufficient that a human is a human, it would be different. I think that the wrong.

We were made to learn about the building of the British Empire by discovery, conquest and treaty. That's the three things that made the backbone of the British Empire. And we know that, we had to know that. And good gracious, some people ask you, 'What part of Africa do you come from?'

Most of us West Indians went to church school and there was discipline there. Back home if you didn't take state exams something was wrong. As you reached a certain age every kid studied for the state exam. We had a good education, most of us.

We're not expecting the West Indian culture to be English culture or African culture. Each person has got their own culture.

When we came here we were invited to come here. We came of our own accord. We paid our own fares and came to England willing. Whereas those in America, they were taken from Africa to America and they had to struggle after the slave trade ended. We emigrated but they were transported. But wherever they are, they want black people to be crushed. They want to crush us. They say we're no good. As if God had made a mistake when he had made us, that he weren't thinking right when he made us. I refuse to accept that. I won't.

There was a time when they were going to give us a ticket and you had to report to a police station.[3] There was a lot of demoralising things that they brought in until a lot of people got their citizenship.[4] But it was a scare at the time.

Really, they've been undermining us all along. Laws have been made to help us but it doesn't change how people are. They make a law but that doesn't say they're going to keep it. They make it to undermine it. I don't know if the conditions will ever change.

Rose Cummings

"I didn't care what colour his skin was"

You see I'm white, but my husband is coloured. Years ago, we went for a drink just in the dinner time. We were asked to leave. 'We don't allow no black men in here', they said. 'He can't stay.'

So we had to get up and go.

We can't understand why this should happen. We look on each other as the same and people don't want to look on you as the same. We don't really understand why these people have got this attitude. The worst thing you could do in that time was for a white girl like me to marry a coloured man. I was brought up decent and I married the man I loved and I didn't care what colour his skin was. I wasn't looking at that.

People treat you real bad, very nasty. We used to go on a bus and they looked down on you like you'd crawled out of a piece of cheese.

I found it hard at the time to cope with two sides.

You Were The Stranger That Came

Rose and Vernal Cummings

Naomi Ramsey

"It goes right through me sometimes"

The discrimination not as bad as before. Like we first came here it was bad, right bad. You'd be walking along and a white body see you and they'll just turn on the other side from you, just like they scorn you.

You go on to a bus and they see you. They don't want you to sit by the side of them. They spread themselves out so you can't sit there. So you don't touch them, don't go near them. Or they get up, get out of the seat and stand up, leave you sitting down. It made us feel rotten.

You just keep it to yourself. When somebody talk to you, you talk back to them. If they don't talk it's up to them. I had that at the hospital all right. I was working on the stroke unit with a lot of oldish people. Sometimes the old people came in and said, 'We don't want no black body to touch us, all right?'

It goes right through me sometimes. It used to go through me. I walked away from them. If they don't want us to touch them then we don't touch them. The Sister would come (she was white). She say to them, 'She is working for us and if you don't want her, you don't want us.'

You had to put up with them. That's how it was then, so that's how I lived with them.

Irene Maddon

"They thought we was a monkey with a tail"

*Y*ou were king and queen in your own community. Here they hassle you and hassle you till you get confused.

You were the stranger that came. I remember if I need someone, I would go to a door and knock and see one of the white people and before you says anything, 'Go away, go away,' they say.

They don't listen to you. 'Get away here from the door. I'll call the police.'

I'm telling you this is all true. Some of them said, 'Oh I can't understand you, I can't understand.'

Some of them even ask you if you speak the same language as them. They're still doing it now. And I says, 'Well, I'm English, I speak the same, English.'

You see there is good and bad and indifferent. You may see three people going along the street here. You say, 'Hello, dear, can I have a word with you, lovey?'

She pass you and she gone, she acts like you're a dog. Or you may rush up and say, 'Hello, mister, can I have a word with you?' and he'll stop and listen to what you have to say. And in some case if you ask, 'Can you direct me to such and such a place, love?' He'll turn back and take you where you're going.

Yes, sometimes people will put themselves out to help you. But they're one in every thousand.

Not all of these white people are bad. Some are very good and some are wicked. My husband told me one evening that he and four friends go out at a pub in Attercliffe and call for a drink at the counter. When they finish with the drink they take back the glass and he saw the man (the manager for the pub) break all four glasses. They didn't say nothing. They went back to the bar for the second drink and they saw the man done the same thing. So the third time they broke the glass themselves and the pub manager saw them broke it and throw it in the bin and he phoned the police. They explained to the police they saw the pub manager break the glass so they did the same. And the policeman says, 'You better go and find yourselves another pub, but don't go back in there.'

I mixed with my people but not white people until I was here long enough. But I always say, 'Hello, you all right?' But that's it. I never goes in their house or stand up and talk to them. I never do while I get used to it in this country.

They didn't have it in their intention for black people to get nothing. They thought when they were recruiting West Indies people to England, we would be all right.

I think to myself that they did thought that we were a slave to come and to clear up all the work and dirty muck while they sit on a bench warm in sunshine and we are a slave to keep them. But when we came they knew that we are human beings.

They thought that we was a monkey with a tail. Because a lot of them said it. All of the white people that we worked with at the Northern General Hospital when I first go there seventeen years ago, they said they thought we did have tail. It's now they realise that we are human beings.

They get better. The racism is still there. Not as much as before though.

5

Pouring Oil On Troubled Water

Our Children And Our Children's Children

Naomi Ramsey

I've worked all the time. You couldn't leave your work because you had to work to maintain your family and keep them going. It's just as bad now but different because the kids wants to work but they can't get no work. They work a short time then nothing. Where can you go from there?

Irene Maddon

*W*ith what I've seen going on these days, I don't think this younger generation has any chance. They have a hard time to go.

They close all the steel firms and all the little factories and all the places where children used to go when they leave school. Now there's nothing there for them. And they go up and down the street, they're doing their shopping, they see things inside. They meet up with friends and break places. They go into prison. That's what the government of this country want, especially with black kids.

Jenny Henry

*W*e want equal treatment but we're not getting it, are we? It's the system that we're living in from schooling to jobs, everything.
If anything happens out on the streets and two whites is

there and two blacks, they'll pick on the blacks. The police come and they hold up the blacks. The white lads, the police they don't touch them. But the black, they'll strip him and they'll do him all sorts because he's black and that's what's going on in the world today. As long as your skin is black you haven't got a chance in England, no chance. [5]

Rose Cummings

"You shouldn't have to take your pedigree to work"

*H*ow can a government who says they are caring turn round and say to a person who won't go on a scheme, 'If you don't go you can't draw no money'? Where do they expect them to get food? I mean, their families can't keep them because they're not working. They're encouraging them to go thieving and do wrong. You know what they say, 'Idle hands are devil hands.' They get into mischief. They're not encouraging them to a decent living, are they?

At one time they used to put it on the door of factories and workshops, 'No more coloureds needed here'. But since the Race Relations Act they've had to take down the notice but they haven't taken out the meaning. What they mean is still there.

We thought as they're born and bred here no matter what colour or race, whether they're Chinese, Japanese, African or Jamaican, whatever they are, it's their own country. They should be able to get a job. But because their skin is black they can't.

My son's gone for hundreds of jobs but two jobs he went for and one of them close down, on this site they were working on. And then he was told to go for another. So he went and this man said he would let him know. He never let him know but he took a white boy because he was going into a select part of Sheffield, which was Dore. Well, my son's good enough to go to Dore whether he's black or white. I mean, you shouldn't have to take your pedigree with you when you go to work, it's your hands you're working with, isn't it?

Ivy Hines

"They feel there's a missing link somewhere with us"

I think if you're coloured and you're going to do anything you must be extra, over–bright, to get anything. What it gives our children is an inferiority complex: 'I am coloured. I can't learn, so what's the use of trying?' That's what some coloured children say. Some coloured children will fight and learn, but some will say, 'I'm not going to get a job because I'm coloured.' It becomes a vicious circle, really.

Some has got work and some hasn't got any. I'm not out there working now. A lot of teenagers has been to school and they been to college and some has got work and some hasn't got anything.

Some of these things are really like pouring oil on troubled water. They give you work for six months and after six months you go back on dole.

I think that it's Hobson's choice that the teenagers have got. Whatever's there you take it, or if you don't take it then you get no money. But each person is a different personality. You got your own identity. You should get your own job. There's no permanent work. You get to work for two years or just six months. The longest is two years and you back on dole. One person come off for six months and another takes that six months. It's like a rotation of crops. There's no permanent jobs now, really. [6]

Pouring Oil On Troubled Water

Harry Barratt and Ivy Hines

6

Nobody Comes And Even Knocks On The Door

Retirement

Nobody Comes And Knocks On The Door

Naomi Ramsey and Ivy Hines, old friends

Naomi Ramsey

"Nobody comes and knocks on the door"

*I*t was a shock, really, to find out that I had a stroke. Up to now I still can't get used to thinking that I can't get out to do me shopping. So it's a big thing, really, but I try to live with it. I try to make the most of it.

I was a very active person. I used to get up, go to work, come back, look after kids, do me housework, go shopping and everything.

After I had me stroke I had to stay in me bedroom all the time. I couldn't go downstairs, into the kitchen. I live in downstairs flat now, everything's there.

I spent twenty years looking after people in the health service and now it's someone's turn to look after me. I do get looked after, they can't do no more. There's a lot of people they have to look after. I get a home help comes in.

There's no friends around where I live. If you're in the house, you're in the house, nobody comes and even knocks at the door. I don't see nobody. I miss all me friends that was at work. We used to talk. We was very close. I had two good friends at work that still come to visit me.

This club helps me, you see. I get out and all the friends I meet here, I can sit down and talk with them. It brings me out of meself. It help me a lot.

Deleta Perkins

"...you got to help somebody"

I get redundancy in '83. I work in factory, never work since. I have to keep busy. I don't like sit down not doing anything. I like to keep busy, me.

I like help people. It give me satisfaction to know that I help somebody. That's the thing my son always says to me, 'Everybody come and call you to do something. Why do you do it?'

I always says to him, just to shut him up, 'Well, I'm so far from home, I don't know who is doing for me mum!' That's the saying back home, 'You don't know where your help is coming from so you got to help somebody.'

Well, when the time comes I got more than I expected. Some people I got help from I don't even know, that's the truth.

Things haven't turned out badly for me. The only thing, I miss me family. I would like to go back home. I've lost my two daughters two years since and they leave their family and really there is nobody to take care of them but me mother. She is seventy seven this year so I have that on my mind, you know. My family is trying to work out something to help me out. I'm just waiting on them. If I live I will have to go back.

I'm here all this time. There are things here that you can

pick up what you wouldn't get at home. You see, I'm here now, not working, I get me money. But if I home now and not working I have to make that for meself so it's different. So I'd miss it but I miss me family more. I would like both but I can't get it both ways.

Ivy Hines

"My mind was obsessed with work"

I have had what you call a premature retirement. I lost twelve years of me livelihood. I was disabled according to circumstances which I had no control over. I had to be registered disabled which compelled me to stop working.

I've been a premature pensioner from when I was forty eight. So it wasn't an easy thing to live with, accustomed to work mornings, afternoons and nights.

I sat and I couldn't move and me mind tell me I'm going to work in the morning. And up to now sometimes I say, 'Oh goodness, I'm going to work, got to go and look for me bags.'

My mind was obsessed with work. I was a workaholic. It wasn't really an easy thing to settle down. But there was something in me that has keep me going up till now. If you got a big mouth and a strong mind... that what keeps me going, really.

That's the worst thing about it, if I wasn't so handicapped I could have gone and done some voluntary work for old folks because I like them. But I can't do anything. I can't even help myself, never mind help anybody else.

The church really is my life, that's what keeps me going. They come and they pick me up for meetings and church services on Sundays. I love the young people at church. I dress like them. I love young folks. I'm really helped by the church and my friends.

My next door neighbour, she don't even know I'm in. I've been in and out of hospital but she don't even know, that's what the flats are. Nobody know where you are. Once you lock that door and go in, nobody sees you, nobody knocks. Sometimes I'm in there for days. You want a bit of fresh air, you open the door and you look out. Anybody passing, you might say hello and that's it. You lock the door and you're in there and it's like a prison in there.

Since I've been poorly this last time I feel I'm in prison. My legs are not well enough to go out on the landing. You just go from the toilet to the television and back to your bed and that's it. [7]

Nobody Comes And Knocks On The Door

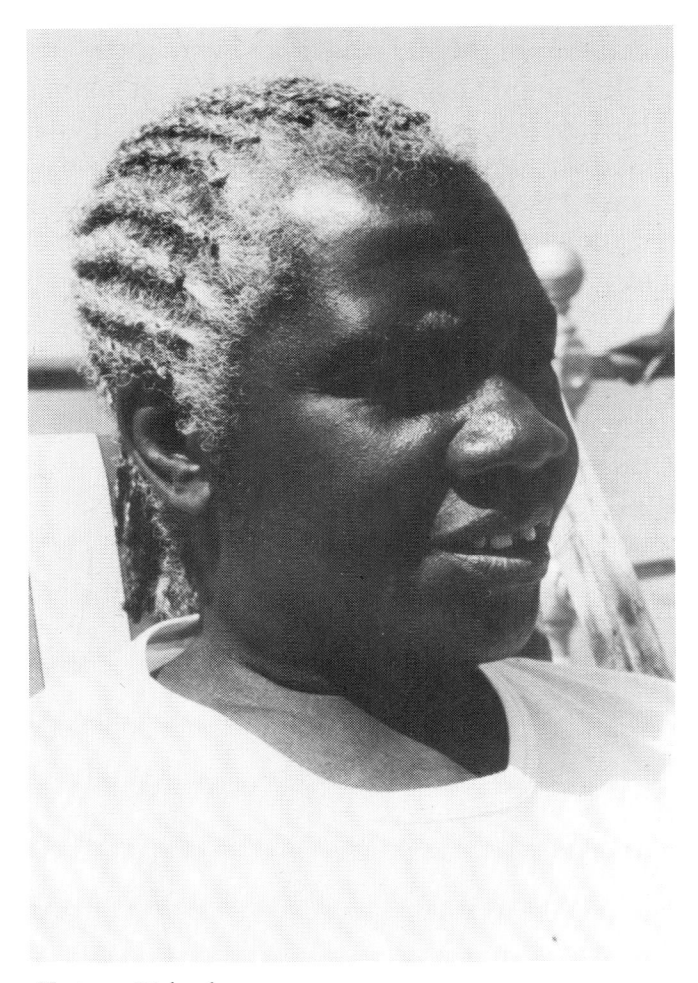

Hortense Richards

Hortense Richards

"It's just a mysterious illness"

The worst ten weeks of my life was spent in hospital. Not because I was treated badly but because of the way my health has treated me. Without a bit of help from people I wouldn't be here now. I couldn't do anything. I couldn't dress myself. I'm just slowly coming back to a bit of a normal life. It's just a mysterious illness. They can't pinpoint what's causing it. I live in daily fear of it. Whenever it comes I'm frightened to do anything. I'm frightened to go in the kitchen. I'm frightened to go upstairs and go to the bathroom. I'm sometimes frightened even to sit in the room and put me clothes on unless somebody is there. It's something that slowly creep up on me. My nerves wasn't always up to scratch. I haven't worked for years and years. I used to work nights at Lodge Moor Hospital. I'm fifty four now and since I was forty six or so I haven't done any real work.

I think loneliness is one of the things because I separated from my husband. I spend most of my time at home. I live with my two sons. Even if you have your children at home you can still be lonely. They don't sit down with you, they don't understand what you need to overcome loneliness. There's nothing to go on with a conversation. Things just build up without you realising it.

I've only just moved over to Sharrow. I lived in Southey Green. There is a few black families up there but not many, they're scattered. It's such a long way out. I didn't like it there, it might have been part of the problem. Apart from family, I never used to have friends coming to see me. Where I am now I got more visitors.

Today the club has got me out and if I don't go out for the rest of the week I can say I been out Monday. The more I go out make me feel better able to cope with things inside the house. I just take each day as it comes.

Ken Baugh

"It's been thirty years since I worked with the soil"

*G*ardening is my big hobby. I used to be an active man, hard working. then I retire, have nothing to do. A friend of mine say, 'Why not start gardening? Get an allotment.'

It's three year I been doing it now and that's what I want to do, just gardening. I love the plants. I like to see them growing, they're beautiful — callaloo, cabbages, scallions, strawberry, raspberry, gooseberry, onions, string beans, kidney beans. My allotment is on Grimesthorpe Road. Everybody is very friendly there.

It's fresh food, you grow it how you want, so you've got healthy food. I started out as a farmer in Jamaica so it's not strange to me. But it's a bit different here, it's hard in this country to farm. You got to put down lime then fertiliser. You can't plant nothing out before May. In Jamaica the soil is more fertile and you start planting straight away in March. There's no special month to plant special things.

It's been about thirty three years since I worked with the soil but I got back to it straight. I work in the steel, gas company and the corporation as well. You just have to adjust yourself to an indoor life, it's no good moaning. But the first chance I get, I go back to working the soil.

7

Home Sweet Home

Going Back

Home Sweet Home

Ken Baugh

Ken Baugh

"I better run off"

I'm from Portland. It's a very nice parish, very fruitful. The most bananas you get is from Portland, and yam, sugarcane, cocoa, coconuts.

We were friendly people from Portland. It's nice to go there when they're selling bananas. I was a United Fruit Company contractor and I used to sell bananas all day on Bunbrook Wharf. I stood and watched them load the ship, people with bananas on their head. There were six, seven or eight ships, as one ship go out another one comes in.

It was a happy life, keeping you fit. We wouldn't get that kind of life in this country. I settle myself down now. I've got three children. I'm getting old and they're young. I want somebody to help me out. But I want to go back. It's a bit more healthier there. I've got a lot to go back for. I left a bit of property there, my farm and house. My brother looks after them.

I stop here and pay the taxes. I can't stop much longer. I better run off.

Naomi Ramsey

"I don't want to go back this way"

I don't think about going back now. Because when I leave home I was eighteen, strong and healthy. The way I am now I don't feel like it. I don't want to go back this way.

In a way England is a good place to be. If I was back home the social security I get here I wouldn't get there in Barbados. But I miss all me family, sunshine and things. I miss a lot. But I've got to put up with it here so that's it. I'm contented with what I have now.

I don't think this society has given me back anything. I don't know, it hasn't given me back nothing really. Because I know I gave them a lot. All that I had, I give to them, but I don't see I got back anything, really, nothing.

Yes, I regret leaving home to come here. But as I'm here I couldn't get back home. I said that when the kids grow up I'll be able to travel to go back if I miss it still. I had a stroke. I'm stuck.

Irene Maddon

"I may be happy outward but I'm not happy inward"

I want to go back. It's my home. My house is there, my sister and brother in law is looking after it. My sisters are there, I am the only one that left and come here.

I always says, 'I may be slow but I'm coming back.' I've been home four times, you know, the last time is August '86. I take the boys that were born here, take them there to show them my country. And when they land in the land of Jamaica, they were shocked. They says, 'Mum, why did you leave this country and go to England?'

I says, 'I like to know different place. You can't sit all the time in your own town. You have to travel and know different people.'

They always say to me, 'Mum, you come here all work, work, work. You never stop. You don't do that in Jamaica.'

I says, 'No, love, you do what you feel like to do. If you don't feel like work today you just sit at home and do home work. If you feel you want to go out and do something for money, well, you do that.'

I've got a lot of experience in this country. Don't get me wrong, I'm not an ungrateful woman. I like it here in some ways but when it comes to the colour bar I hate that. I think all of us are one people. We're all God's children.

From the start I never had that intention to stop here forever. 'Home, sweet home'. No matter if I'm getting a thousand pounds a day, at the back of my mind is still my country. I may be happy outward but I'm not happy inward. I'm going back home if it pleases the Lord.

I get nothing. I've been here thirty years and I have to work. The only thing I get from living in this country is since I've been coming to this club.

Rastan Reynolds

"I would like to go back to Jamaica but I can't"

I can't go upstairs now. I can't go downstairs. My house got three floors. I live on me own and is a big house and I get a bit lonely, man. Sometime I sit in me house and cry, all alone and nobody to stop with me.

The pub not far. Sometimes I crawl along. I like to go there, I have a few friends in there.

I would like to go back to Jamaica but can't. I have a better home here than what I would have in Jamaica. Me house in Jamaica was only two rooms. I couldn't afford to buy a big house in Jamaica.

Oscar Noel Phillip

"Little England"

*B*arbados is very good, it's smashing. They call it another 'Little England'. I miss it a lot. I really miss it every day, even now. I want to go. It's not a place like home here, you know. I'm not at home.

Val Haslam and Vernon Colleymore who run the lunch club

NOTES

[1] (Page 49) State Enrolled Nurses were known as "green frocks" because of their uniform. Many Caribbean women hoped to train as nurses when they came to Britain but found that they were unable to.

The National Health Service has long been a substantial employer of black people. But evidence has shown that this employment is generally concentrated in lower status occupations and grades within the service.

In 1987 Sheffield Health Authority conducted a survey from a sample of around five thousand employees across all occupations. One of the findings showed that ethnic minorities were almost three times more likely to be found in the low status Auxiliary Nursing grade than white people.

A second study of all qualified nurses in the employment of the authority showed that "ethnic minority nurses were disproportionately concentrated in the less prestigious medical specialism, that this concentration was re-inforced by the enrolment pattern for post–basic qualification courses, and that in recent years there appeared to be a significant fall off in the recruitment of young nurses from ethnic minority backgrounds."

Race and Employment in Sheffield District Health Authority by P. Gibbon, July 1990
Unpublished report commissioned by Sheffield's Department of Employment and Economic Development and Sheffield's Council for Racial Equality

[2] (Page 61) Many thousands of people in Sheffield have lost their homes through the slum clearance programmes of the 1960s and 1970s. Often people were offered only a few hundred pounds for the compulsory purchase of their homes. Black families concentrated in areas like Pitsmoor, Burngreave, Tinsley and Attercliffe were disproportionately affected and often found it hard to find out what their rights and entitlements were.

[3] (Page 70) Ivy cannot remember the details of these rumoured regulations but it is clear that the black community was closely monitored by the authorities in the 1950s. "In Sheffield, for example,

NOTES

the Chief Constable had deputed two police officers to "...... observe, visit and report on" the black population. A card index was compiled, listing the names, addresses, nationalities and places of employment of the city's five hundred and thirty four black inhabitants."

From an unpublished paper on the views of black citizens in the 1950s

[4] (Page 70) The first Commonwealth Immigrants Act of 1962 was a clearly racist piece of legislation designed to restrict the entry of black Commonwealth settlers. British citizens with passports issued outside the UK were subject to entry control. People now needed to obtain employment vouchers graded according to the skills required by the British labour market. They were also now liable to deportation if convicted of an offence within five years of arrival.
"Blackness was officially equated with second–class citizenship, with the status of undesirable immigrant."

Peter Fryer, **Staying Power — The History of Black People in Britain**

[5] (Page 81) According to findings from the British Crime Survey published in September 1990, Afro–Caribbeans, along with males generally, were the group most likey to be stopped by the police. The report concludes,
"A clear picture emerges from the factors examined here; the police are more likely to stop and question young, single, unemployed, Afro–Caribbean males."
Afro–Caribbeans are also more likely than either whites or Asians to be searched as a result of being stopped. Thirty four per cent were searched in traffic stops and thirty six per cent in pedestrian stops, compared with nine per cent and twenty per cent of whites and fourteen and twenty five per cent of Asians.
The report also notes that Afro–Caribbeans were significantly less likely than others to be told why they were stopped.

Runnymede Trust Bulletin, *November 1990, No. 240*

NOTES

[6] (Page 84) High unemployment over the last ten years has hit the black community hardest. Since 1981, white unemployment has increased by a third in the region, but amongst Afro–Caribbean people the rate of increase has been over one half. Afro–Caribbean people are twice as likely to be unemployed as white people.
Young black people are the hardest hit in the job market. In 1986, only twenty one of five hundred and twenty five black school leavers had found work by December.
In December, 1989, figures suggested that white fifth years were nearly three times more likely than black fifth years to enter employment. Fewer white fifth formers were unemployed compared with 1985, but twice as many black fifth years were unemployed as were in 1985.
Of all those school leavers who left the full–time educational system in 1987, 15.9% of white leavers were unemployed and 42.9% of black leavers were out of work.
Young black people on Youth Training Schemes are far less likely to find work on leaving than white trainees. Black trainees are also less represented on "LCU" schemes (Large Company Unit Schemes — workplace/employer based with the highest likelihood of employment). For *all* Youth Training Scheme leavers in Sheffield, only 59% of whites, 36% of African/Caribbean and 25% of Asian people are employed.
These statistics explain the lack of confidence that many black and ethnic minority young people have in the YTS programme.

Information from the following reports produced by Sheffield's Department of Employment and Economic Development and Race Equality Unit:

Estimations of Black People's Unemployment in Sheffield, D. Sequerra and M. Atkins, 1987
Black Young People, Unemployment and YTS
Young People, Racism and the Labour Market, D. Sequerra and M. Atkins, 18th December 1989
What Happens After YTS? Destinations of Black and White Youth Training Graduates in Sheffield, M. Atkins

[7] (Page 93) After spending twenty years on Kelvin Flats, Ivy now lives in a single level flat on the eleventh floor of Crawshaw block on the Netherthorpe Estate. She is much more comfortable now.